York Courses pr

CW00497561

THE PSAL
prayers for today

CD Track [1]

Hello, I'm Simon Stanley of York Courses and I'm delighted to be your guide through the contributions of our distinguished speakers; contributions which form an integral part of this course, alongside the booklet written by Stephen Cottrell. And here is Bishop Stephen to introduce his course.

SC: When you don't know what to pray. When you're not sure how to make sense of a situation or an emotion. When anger is suppressed or joy restrained. When life is confusing or painful, the psalms are there for you. They are the prayer book of the Bible. We love them because they're so old, prayed by the people of God for generations. *And* we love them because they're so young! They are the prayers of the people of God in their youth. That's why they are so full of vigour, energy, passion. If you're feeling fed up, there is always a psalm that's more fed up than you. If you're feeling frustrated, there's a psalm that's more frustrated than you. If you're feeling joyful, there's a psalm that's more joyful than you. The psalms are a library of praise and petition. They provide words when we don't have any words. They are there for us to inhabit, recite and build our prayers upon. They are a template for expressing who we are and all that we think and feel in the presence of God and they provide wisdom for navigating our way through the challenges and delights of life. I find as I get older that my own praying is simpler and starker. Often I feel I want nothing more than a psalm and the silence before God that it leads me into.

So this course will introduce you to the psalms as God's offer of words to shape your praying, words so poignant and precise that Jesus turned to them as he hung upon the cross.

This is timely, because so many of the spiritual and liturgical disciplines which were part of Christian formation for our forebears have fallen into disuse. So for instance, the idea of reading prayers and learning things by heart is out of fashion. One of the axioms of our age is that somehow prayer can only be heartfelt if it is extempore. The Old Testament is read less and less in church; and whereas in former times the biblical diet of worship always included a psalm, in some churches they are hardly read at all. But by learning to love the psalms, by using them in our prayer and worship, and perhaps even by learning one or two by heart, we will be giving ourselves a present that will last a lifetime. And will be there for us at the hour of our death.

[2] Let me briefly introduce the speakers to you. John Bell is a minister of the Church of Scotland whose ministry has been wide and distinguished in many spheres: liturgy, music, broadcasting, campaigning, and as a speaker and preacher in great demand. He's a member of the Iona Community.

Rose Hudson-Wilkin is the first ever female Chaplain to the House of Commons and is also Vicar of a Church of England parish in Hackney, North London. She is a chaplain to the Queen and a prebendary of St Paul's Cathedral.

Jane Leach, who does the reflections at the end of each session, is a Methodist minister and Principal of Wesley House, Cambridge, offering many courses and opportunities for study.

Timothy Radcliffe is a Roman Catholic priest and Dominican friar. A renowned theologian, his writing and speaking is valued for its clarity and accessibility. He's an Honorary Doctor of Divinity at the University of Oxford.

All four are contributors to Radio 4's Thought for the Day.

So, introductions over, let's begin.

1

THE PSALMS Session 1:

CD Track [3]

PSALM 100 – KNOW THAT THE LORD IS GOD

'O, be joyful in the Lord, all the earth. Enter his gates with thanksgiving.' So these are the two themes of Psalm 100: joy and thanksgiving. I asked our three experts if worship brings them joy – or is a duty to perform. First John Bell, then Timothy Radcliffe, and finally Rose Hudson-Wilkin.

JB: Worship is both. I think we owe God honour and obedience and praise, because we don't take lightly the world that we have and the life that we have. So there is an element of duty, but the duty is not an arduous thing. And joy, certainly, because it's not a solitary engagement. You're there with other people, and Psalm 100 is a corporate psalm – it's not an individual psalm. So there is something very pleasurable about singing to God in the company of other people.

TR: Usually it brings me joy, but often it's a slog. We go into the chapel and pray here four times a day, and sometimes I have no recollection what on earth has happened at all. But I think any deep joy probably requires long periods of slog.

RHW: Oh no, it must never be a duty. Coming from the Caribbean, worship is joyful – it is passionate. And it's been very difficult adjusting to a community that shows no passion in its worship.

[4] Thinking about worship generally, it's worth asking, as a child might, what is worship? Timothy, John, and then Rose.

TR: You remember Noel Coward famously meeting a friend after a long time, and he said to his friend: 'We haven't got time to talk about both of us, so let's talk about *me*.' And I think that's very often how we live. We're the centre of the world. But when we go to worship, we get carried out of ourselves, and God becomes the centre – at least from little moments. And that is a vast liberation. Because also, when we go to worship in church we go to be with other people. We go to join a community – and that carries us out of ourselves in another way. So, I think part of what worship is about is self-forgetfulness in the presence of God.

JB: We spend time with people whom we love. And we do that because spending time is a sign of love. We give time to what's important. And so, when we go to worship God, we go as a group of people, all of whom believe that God's important. And we go to spend time with God, and to share with God the things that are important in our lives, and to hear from God the things that are important for us to understand.

RHW: Worship is our offering of praise and thanksgiving to God. You know, we go through life, and worship affords us that moment when we pause and acknowledge that greater force beyond us. And I'm often seen here around in Parliament, and on the tubes – or elsewhere – singing, as I go along. Because there is this real sense of awareness of this great, fantastic God, who makes my life possible – and all the things around it.

[5] *Okay, a youngster may say, you sing hymns and stuff, and that all makes you feel better to help you get on with your own comfortable little life. So what? John.*

JB: I don't think that worship should ever be seen as something which is primarily aimed at being a kind of therapeutic exercise for those who engage in it. Because the focus of worship is God, and not ourselves. And in any relationship that we have, with anybody at all, being at the peak of our emotional high is not something we can sustain. And when things have gone wrong, and when things are troubling, then you share that with the one that you love. So, public worship has to have within it – yes, a time when people can, if it's appropriate, feel exuberant, but also a time when other emotions can be expressed, and questions can be asked, and hard things can be pondered.

Timothy takes a slightly different line.

TR: Most worship, if you're attentive, is potentially very disconcerting. It doesn't let you get on with your comfortable life. That's why C S Lewis resisted conversion. Because he knew that if he attended to the Lord, then his life would be turned upside-down. So that, when he finally turned to the Lord – at Magdalene College here in Oxford – he said, 'I was the most dejected convert in England that day.'

And Rose.

RHW: If our worship does not connect with our everyday lives then we are probably barking up the wrong tree. If our worship does not inform us, does not inspire us, does not change us in the way we respond to others around us, then perhaps it's not worship. So when we say that last prayer: 'Send us out in the power of the Spirit to live and work to your praise and your glory', there has to be a connect.

[6] *In the booklet Stephen Cottrell writes: 'my praise of God not only expands my love of God, but my ability to love the world and to inhabit the world with a thankful heart', just as Rose was saying. How can we 'serve the Lord with gladness', as the Psalm suggests we should? Rose, then John, then Timothy.*

RHW: When I talk about being joyful, or having gladness or – you know – praise and thanksgiving, it doesn't mean 'noise'. I can't cope with noise. And so the joy and the gladness comes from doing the will of God, and living out the will of God. That brings joy and gladness. And that, in effect, then gets shared with those around us.

JB: When people talk about serving the world with gladness, sometimes the spectre emerges in the minds of very cautious people that that means clapping your hands, and shouting and – shouting hallelujahs, and showing a strong effort to try to please God – as if God were come – were some kind of, benign but rather sad old man in the sky, and you have to kind of, you know, rouse him with a tickling stick on a Sunday morning when the congregation gets together. Serving God with gladness is doing the things which God requires of us, with an open heart. With appreciation for what God has done, and ensuring that the will of God is done on the earth. So discipleship isn't a grudge thing. So we serve the Lord with gladness when we enjoy being disciples – and when we do that with a sense of privilege and anticipation that new things are going to happen.

TR: The gladness that we have in the Lord is not just, I think, an emotion – you know: love Jesus because he's absolutely wonderful. That sort of happy-clappy joy, I think, often does not endure. But joy that we have is God. Because God is joy. God's life is unutterable, overflowing, endless joy. So you couldn't serve the Lord without gladness, because that would be to reject something that is – is at the very core of the life of God, which is the joy of the father in the son, and the joy of the son in the father, which is the Spirit.

[7] *'The Lord is gracious, his faithfulness endures from generation to generation.' But does history reveal God's faithfulness? What about the holocaust that destroyed faith for so many Jewish people, and other people too? What about our own, much smaller, trials and tribulations? Where is God's faithfulness then? John and Timothy.*

JB: I believe that we have to get round the idea – well, not get round the idea, *dismiss* the idea, that faith in God means that we will *always* feel the sun shining on our face; our heart will *always* be strangely warmed; and we'll *never* be affected by bitterness, by misfortune or by disaster. We have to be adults in the Christian faith and not children. I mean, when I say that, I mean we have to be adults and not childish. It's a childish expectation that you'll get what you want, and that your parent will always give you what you think you deserve. It's an adult relationship, which realises that we live in a world where bad things happen to good people. And faith is not an insurance policy against that. Faith is what enables you to deal with what's hard, because you believe that, if the worst happens, the best through God will still be to come.

TR: Elie Wiesel, when he was in Auschwitz, recalls having to watch the death of three people being hanged – and one of them was a child. And he watched the body of the child twitching as it died slowly, and he heard somebody behind him say: 'Where is God? Where is God now?' and Elie Wiesel heard, like a voice inside him, say: 'There is God – he's hanging on the gibbet.' So God's faithfulness is not that he's fixing things for us all the time. He's not like a faithful butler. God's faithfulness is that he is with us. The image I have is: you see a friend on the other side of the room, and you smile at her, and you see all of her, and then she advances towards you, and you give her a great big hug. And now you can see only a little bit of her – you can just see her face. You give her a great big kiss. For a moment, you glimpse her lips, and then you don't see anything at all. And the closer you get to God, it always passes through these moments of loss. The atheist thinks of the loss as the disappearance of God, but we know it, ultimately, as intimacy. He disappears from our awareness, from our perception, because he's closer.

Rose speaks out of the experience of her Jamaican family.

RHW: Do you know, I often say that I learnt my theology from my parents' and grandparents' generation, because there you see a people – and actually from the history of my own people – there you see a people downtrodden, kicked, but here they were, not out. And here they were, actually recognising that God is *their* God. And they had an enormous amount of trust in him. And, you know, if they can trust God and recognise God as faithful – be the one sure thing that they can depend on when all else around them is failing – then I want that too.

[8] *And now, for her reflection on the first session, we welcome Jane Leach.*

This psalm always reminds me of the words of Jesus when he tells the Pharisees that if his disciples were silent, the rocks and stones themselves would cry out. There is an exuberance in the joyful noise made by the whole created order that is infectious and that invites those who know that the Lord is God to join in.

There seems to be nothing specific that prompts this song of praise, other than a delight in the nature of God's very self whose steadfast love and enduring faithfulness have surely been experienced by the author. And so delighted is the author that he orchestrates the whole earth and the whole congregation, commanding us to worship, to come, to know, to enter, to give thanks and to bless God's name.

There's an ecstasy about this kind of praise that takes us out of ourselves; transcends despair; overrides arrogance and overcomes anxiety. For in the act of praise, we are never the focus, instead we are blessedly released from the tyranny of being at the centre of our own concerns as we are transported by God's dazzling goodness.

There are many ways to become 'lost in wonder, love and praise' – in the silence of the Quaker meeting; in the glory of the Orthodox liturgy; in the singing of a great hymn, but if our corporate worship is to be more than dead convention, somehow we need to be leading one another into this deeply dazzling place.

THE PSALMS Session 2:

CD Track [9]

PSALM 130 – OUT OF THE DEPTHS HAVE I CRIED

More than once in this psalm we read about waiting for the Lord. What does is mean, to 'wait for the Lord'? Rose Hudson-Wilkin, and then Timothy Radcliffe.

RHW: You don't need to rush into this. You don't need to get the answer to this problem right now. Just wait. It will all be revealed. I have to trust God that he is going to deliver. I love, in the Old Testament, when Elijah was in hiding in the cave, and God discovers him, and says: What on earth are you doing here? And he says: I'm the only one left. And God says: Of course you're not, don't be silly! But there is all the, the earthquake and various – you know, really noisy – woahh – things happening. And God is not in those. And then there is the still, small voice. And God is to be found in that stillness.

TR: Why is waiting important? I think it's because the Lord gives himself, as a gift, and every gift has to come at the right moment. So that, if I were to pray, for example, for great holiness to come upon me, actually, this will be a lifelong project. And the Lord will give me the grace, as I need it, and when I need it.

John Bell has an interesting example.

JB: There is one person who I once had great difficulty with. I couldn't like this person at all. And we had to work fairly close with each other. And it seemed that there was was a constant impediment, and I would pray to God: 'please make him more co-operative.' Well, you know, I prayed that for about three months – I should have become an atheist because nothing was happening! And then came a day when, in a meeting, he said something which was not contradicting what I had said, but which was extremely helpful. And then, two or three weeks later, there was another opportunity where he said something which was contrary to my expectations, and which helped move things on a bit. And I was able to thank him for what he had contributed. And after that, the relationship that I had with this person changed completely, because I had not been given a changed Robert, but I had been given an opportunity to see a side of him which hitherto I didn't want to notice. You know – the generous, the insightful, the helpful thing. And – and for me, that's been always a moment that I return to when I don't get what I want when I pray.

[10] *Verse 2 of Psalm 130 tells us that God doesn't keep a record of sins. But we tend to turn this on its head, thinking that he keeps a record of all the good things we do, in the hope that we gather more good points than negative ones, thus securing salvation. John.*

JB: The psalm doesn't actually say that God *does* keep a tally. It says, *if* you were to do this, then none of us would actually – manage to pass the test. But I really rail against the notion that God's primary passion is in counting the sins of people who have done things wrong. That is a heavenly tyrant. That's not a loving, gracious creator.

[11] *How can we move from the record-keeping image to relying on God's grace and forgiveness, as expressed in verses 2 and 3? Timothy, and Rose.*

TR: In the Bible, of course, the one who keeps a note of everything is Satan. Satan is the one who notes all your deeds – observing, and noting everything down. Thomas Aquinas – who I have to mention as a Dominican – Thomas Aquinas said: the really virtuous acts are done with spontaneity, because they spring from who you are. You don't do things that are meritorious because you *should*, but because you like to. In our society, our moralistic society, we tend to think of it the other way round: that the meritorious act is the one that you do with great difficulty – going against the grain. Aquinas would say: that's okay at an early stage, but real virtue, which just means strength – inner strength – means that you spontaneously and happily do the good, because it's wonderful to do it.

RHW: I'm often reminded of the passage from First Corinthians, which says, love does not keep a record of wrongs. And I am tempted to do that, because I say to my husband, 'don't drop your clothes on the floor' and he says, 'oh, I didn't do that'. And I hear myself say, 'okay, I'm going to make a little note of when you do it so I can remind you later.' And then this passage of scripture, you know, hits me: Love does not keep a record of wrong. So we don't. You let go. And that takes some learning. To let go, and trust.

[12] *The Bible, on the whole, encourages us to trust God, and to love God. But here, in verse 4, the psalmist also talks about fearing God. What does it mean to fear God? John, and then Rose, and Timothy.*

JB: This notion that we should be terrified of God has to be balanced by the sense that when we are confronted with one who loves us, and who is willing, if we but acknowledge where we've failed, to forgive us and let that be past, that is an incredibly awesome thing. And if we don't feel apprehensive in the presence of that grace, then there's something wrong with us.

RHW: When I was a little girl growing up, we truly respected adults – we really did. There was a trust relationship there, but there was real respect. So there are things that we would say to each other, but we wouldn't say it in the presence of an adult, because we just knew that it was not appropriate. Sadly, we've lost that in society today. And because we've lost it in terms of how we treat adults, I think we've probably lost it somewhat in terms of how we treat God, and we relate to God. We've begun sort of treating God as if he's just your – in Jamaican language – 'yard boy' [*laughing*] or your 'bro'. He's not your 'bro'! So yes, I think I fear God. And for me, that is about respecting God.

TR: In the *Narnia* tales by C S Lewis, if you remember, Susan asks Beaver, of Aslan the lion: is he safe? And the beaver replies: who said anything about safe? But he's good. And I think the Lord's like that. It's a thoroughly dangerous thing to get involved with God, because he might ask you to do extraordinary things. Turn your life upside-down. So we should fear the Lord. It's not the cringing fear that we'd have of somebody who's opposed to us – hostile to us. But it's the – the trepidation of somebody who will give us everything. And make us utterly different from what we were before.

[13] *Stephen Cottrell writes in the booklet that the psalms 'give permission for my joy to be exuberant, my frustration to be uninhibited and my anger to be released'. Joy and frustration, yes – but what place does anger have in the Christian life? Timothy, and John.*

TR: St Augustine said that anger was one of the two daughters of Hope, and that if you're angry, at least it shows that you think things might change. If you become utterly despairing, you probably won't be angry. You'll just be deflated. And so anger is very promising. It means that you want to *do* something.

JB: Anger can be a creative thing. And to give anger a negative connotation is to misunderstand that emotion. You know, when anger comes from jealousy, then it's not the kind of thing we want to hold on to. But when anger comes out of a belief that something is wrong and that it has to be righted; when anger is the spur to enabling justice or mercy or compassion to be made evident, then anger is a creative thing.

[14] *I wondered if Timothy was often angry.*

TR: I've lived in many war situations – in Rwanda and Burundi and Angola

and – and when you see the brutality of war, then your anger is stirred. And rightly so. But just as the enemy – so-called – may kill and mutilate people, because he, or she, is only seeing them as objects, the danger is that your anger could do just the same thing to them.

[15] *Not just anger for Rose, but rage.*

RHW: We should be *enraged* at the young woman who was raped in India. And we should be *enraged*, and angry, at the continued unjust treatment of those who are seen as lower caste. We should be *enraged* at what is happening in Ukraine. Boko Haram behaviour, abducting all those children. The world has thrown their arms up in despair. The United Nations is now full of guns and, you know, I am *enraged* about those things. And what that rage does is it allows me to hold this up before God.

[16] *Stephen also asserts in the booklet that vengeance stirs within all of us. Is he right? Do any of our contributors feel or justify vengeance? John, Timothy, and Rose.*

JB: It would be extraordinary if we didn't feel vengeful, or a desire for revenge. And there's a whole lot – a whole lot of the psalms which indicate that that is a human emotion. But – but look, anger is not a thing to hold on to, you know, it has to be let go of, or sublimated, or somehow worked out. And for me, one of the interesting things is that repeatedly in the psalms, when people will vengeance on another people, they put it in God's hands. There's no psalm that says: God give me the time and the gun and I'll deal with the person. Always – repeatedly in the psalms – where vengeance is an expression – an experience which people are having, they put that in the hands of God. And, you know, Paul takes that over when he says: 'vengeance is mine, says the Lord and I will repay.' It's not – we can feel it, but it's not us to act on it. It's not ours to act on it.

TR: Oh yes, I think it's always there, you know – the little temptation to vengeance, even if it's only a very small act. Somebody takes my favourite mug, you know, and I'll jolly well make sure that they won't get an extra portion for supper this evening. But it's – because vengeance in that sense is really captivity. You're allowing yourself to be captivated – to be the pawn of what other people do. And one is only really free and spontaneous, I think, when you're liberated from the mechanisms of vengeance.

RHW: Vengeance is not healthy. It is certainly not healthy. I think it was Desmond Tutu who, when he was told: what about the scripture passage which says an eye for an eye and a tooth for a tooth, he said: we'll all be toothless and blind if we stick to that [*laughing*]. So, so no. Being angry – yes. But I think, because we are the people of God, we need to, to dig really deeply.

[17] *And now over to Jane for her reflection.*

It is no surprise that this psalm is a favourite of Christians because it's one of the seven psalms identified by Luther for penitential use. Unlike some psalms that blame God or enemies for what's gone wrong, in this psalm the author takes responsibility for the breach in the relationship with God, confesses and waits humbly for God to speak. There's a trust expressed in this psalm that is quite breathtaking. Despite the belief sometimes articulated that it is only the voice of the righteous that will be heard on high, here the author dares to ask for God's attention despite a deep awareness of his own faults.

For anyone who has ever needed to ask forgiveness for an action that has the power to destroy a relationship, perhaps the tension in this psalm might be lost. It's one thing to know the character of the person you hope will forgive you; it's another thing to wait for them to respond once you have told them the worst.

The psalmist confesses and then must wait, and wait, for God to speak.

What God says in the silence of the psalmist's heart or perhaps in the voice of the priest in absolution is not recorded, and yet somewhere between verse 6 and verse 7 hope turns to assurance.

Conscious throughout of God's nature as a God of steadfast love; a God of redemption; a God of forgiveness, in the end, it's only the action of God that can heal the gulf and turn our tears into a dance.

THE PSALMS Session 3:

PSALM 13 – HOW LONG, O LORD?

The writer of Psalm 13 laments because he's waited on the Lord, and God seems to be hiding his face. I asked Timothy Radcliffe, John Bell and Rose Hudson-Wilkin if they ever feel that God is distant or absent, and how they – and we – might cope with these feelings.

TR: Many of the great saints have, what you might call, dark nights of the soul. I think it's God's particularly resilient children who probably have those. I just manage the occasional grey evening! I lose a sense that God is the great joy at the centre of creation. But then, you hang in, and you endure. What one of the most beautiful words, I think, in John's Gospel is 'abide'. Jesus says he will *abide* with us. And sometimes we just have to *abide* with him, as we wait to recover that sense of – of his sparkling vitality.

JB: Sometimes when people feel that God's absent, or God isn't responding, it's maybe because they've left God behind. Now, let me think of one particular person, who would say, at the moment that, you know, he's waiting for God to turn up. And God isn't turning up: 'How long, O Lord?' And my suspicion is that about eight years ago, when this person's mother died, he felt suddenly the absence of his mother. And he's felt that ever since. And he hasn't either forgiven God about it, or really, kind of, mentioned it in prayer. I don't think he prays. And I think the way he has

to go do – what he has to do is to go back to the moment when he began to feel that separation, and maybe deal with his grief. Because I don't think that he's really dealt with his grief. A lot of the time agnosticism, when it creeps in, comes – or is rooted in – an experience which we have not opened up and been honest about. But we've kind of left it as a kind of doubt – as something over which a curtain has been drawn. And maybe we need to pull the curtain apart, and revisit that experience, and find God where we left him.

RHW: This Psalm in particular which, you know, which is crying out to God, it's basically saying: 'where the hell are you?' You know: 'I'm in this predicament, where are you? I need your help.' And I think there are times in our lives where we feel that God might not be listening – he's not acting as fast as we want him to act. It might be in the case of someone being very ill, someone who is dying and, you know, you are saying: 'I need you to save this person.' We are not put in a box, a cushioned box, to prevent us having those moments when we cry out to God.

[19] I asked Timothy, Rose and John if they had any words of encouragement for those who are going through a dark spiritual time.

TR: In my tradition as a Catholic, we do have a tradition of asking people to pray with us. You know, you want a friend of yours to be healed, or you want to pass an exam – whatever it is – and you say: 'pray for me please.' And I think it's very important that you pray – we pray for each other. And even sometimes *with* each other. That helps us to keep us going in the tough moments. When I was flying to Iraq, I had a seven-hour wait in Istanbul airport, which is more than I think anybody should have to endure! [*Laughing.*] But after about three hours I was joined by one of my Iraqi brethren, and then an hour later by one of my American brethren, and the three of us waited together. And then the time passes much more quickly – and I think it's just the same when you're waiting for God to answer your prayers. Not to do it alone, but to share the waiting with other people.

RHW: For those moments I look to Job. I look to Job. Job, who was stripped of everything, and yet Job was able to say, 'I know that my redeemer liveth.' And so there is a sense in which, when one is going through that barren moment, you have got to find that one hook to hold on to, so that you are not left devastated.

JB: When the writer talks about trusting God, it is saying, that in the midst of this feeling of abandonment, I still believe that, that you will come into my life – that days will be better. I hang on to that, because I don't want to hang on to despair. And I'm moving the needle from pointing to rejection and misfortune, to the possibility of hope and fulfilment and completeness and understanding. So, for me, in this context salvation is when we are ultimately able to understand what has happened in the past, and to see that God has worked through it and that the sun will shine again. And, you know, we have to live in that hope. Otherwise we just become embittered.

[20] *In verses 5 and 6 of this psalm the psalmist expresses, in stark contrast to the first four verses, wonderful, positive sentiments. What are we to make of this juxtaposition of apparent spiritual opposites? Timothy and Rose.*

TR: When my father was dying I had to fly home from Jerusalem and go pretty well directly to the hospital. And all of his six children, we were all gathered around the bed with my mother, and I hadn't got the usual prayer book, so I just took out my breviary and we passed the Psalms around. And they were the perfect psalms with which to face death, because you bring to word your anger, your distress, your sorrow. It's legitimate to feel like this, but then the psalm carries you through to the joy. It's like – it's like a surfer, you know – you climb on the wave and it carries you through.

RHW: I look at my own life, growing up in a very – growing up in poverty in Jamaica. I think my faith has saved me, I really do. And it has saved me in a way that – here I am now, with – someone with great confidence, which I would not have had, I don't think, without, without my faith. And so I can understand this sort of juxtaposition – the on the one hand crying out, but on the other hand actually saying, you know, 'I'm in your hands, Lord, and, you know, I'm going to be okay.'

[21] *John wants us to be more aware of what the psalms are, and what they're not.*

11

JB: We have to stop thinking of the psalms as just speaking for us to God. I mean, the one psalm is about love and adoration, another psalm's about rejection. What we have to appreciate is that the psalms are the record of different people as they encounter God, and as they related their experiences to God. And if we cannot ascend to the sentiment in a psalm, maybe we're not supposed to. But maybe we're supposed to allow that psalm to take us into the mind and the experience of people for whom the light has turned to darkness – or God seems to be absent. Into the experience of exile, as in Psalm 137, where people wish great vengeance on their enemies; into the experience of profound depression, as in Psalm 88 – and the psalm then becomes a means of interceding for other people. So I believe that the psalms give us a vocabulary for joy. I believe they give us a vocabulary for pain. But we shouldn't feel that in our devotional life every one of these words must mean something to us. Rather, I think, we allow those that *can* speak for us at different times to speak, and those that can't speak for us to be the means by which we pray for others.

[22] *So, we can't abandon the psalms – but how do we use them to get the best out of them? How are we to cope with the stuff that seems so at odds with the Christian Gospel? The violence, the ungenerous thoughts, all the whingeing and the 'poor me' in them. Perhaps Timothy can help us with this.*

TR: I've been saying psalms now since I joined the Order – which is almost fifty years ago – four times a day. And so they've become a very important part just of my life. And sometimes they're boring. And sometimes you say a whole psalm without registering a single word that it's about. But often enough, they engage you. Now, it's true they can be a bit whingey sometimes. It's true they can go on and on and on about 'poor old me' – and this can be a little bit irritating. Sometimes even self-indulgent, you might feel. But we do it. Our religion is extremely realistic about what human beings are like – and this is what human beings are like! Often we do get wrapped up in 'poor little me' and self-pity, and – and it's good that when we see it there we recognise that that's something that's part of our own experience too. And if we smile at the psalmist for doing it, we may even learn to smile at ourselves for doing it.

Rose is pretty pragmatic.

RHW: When people say to me, 'oh, you know, there's violence, there's this, that, the other', and I'm saying, 'hang on a minute, there's violence in the world. Are you going to stop being in the world?' I think it's a cop-out, frankly, it's a real cop-out. You know, we don't stop living because things isn't right with the world. We do our best to live right, and to show the world that there can be a different way. So I think it's a real cop-out when we go in the other direction.

[23] Before this session's reflection, a last personal word from John Bell about the apparently absent God in the face of sadness and loss.

JB: My mother died after a cruel illness. A beautiful woman. And the ability of me to deal with this having, you know, been in the pastoral ministry at different times in my life, was negligible. I couldn't understand what was happening to her. But then, you have to appreciate that the life we are given is not a life that comes with guarantees. Nobody in the Bible gets it easy. Nobody, from Moses to John the Divine; Moses is a murderer, John the Divine is living in exile. And everybody in between, whom God calls, has to deal with the fact that the life we are given does not come with guarantees. And that, if there should be a hideous illness, if, as in the case of one of my friends, a child should be given drugs and they die, if somebody should lose a job, it's not because there is a malign being in heaven who is turning the channels of mercy away from us, so that we can feel harm and become better people. It's just that life sometimes goes into the doldrums, that there are fault lines in the physical universe, and there are fault lines in the fabric of each of us. And we have to be mature and accept that.

[24] *And now, Jane's reflection on this session.*

There's no polite preamble to psalm 13. The situation is urgent. The plea has been made before. God has already been questioned and has not answered; a touch of impatience or even despair is entering the tone, 'How long, O Lord? Will you forget me forever?'

The wisdom of pouring out our grief and anger is something that contemporary bereavement studies has underlined, and we know that the terminal patients that do best are those who express their fears and frustrations to someone who can listen. Yet, this, and other psalms that use even more extreme language, the Christian tradition has neglected – leaving out the angry verses and certainly not praying them. But why not?

Perhaps some of us have genuinely lived the kind of lives that have never left us vengeful and hurt or humiliated; perhaps some of us have assumed that if there's a problem it's our own fault; perhaps, deep down, some of us don't really believe that speaking to God or anyone else makes any difference, not realising that the choice to suppress our feelings can leave us isolated and depressed.

The psalms of lament offer a vibrant alternative. Risking being overwhelmed by our feelings on the one hand, and being dropped by the one we hope will listen on the other, we are encouraged here to take our courage in our hands and dare God to deal with the worst of what we're experiencing. Whilst friends and family might fear and fly, the God of the psalms honours his promise to meet his people.

THE PSALMS Session 4:

PSALM 23 – YOU SPREAD A TABLE BEFORE ME

Here's the psalm many of us could recite by heart. Beloved of royal weddings, frequently used at funerals, and full of sheep – what's not to like?! Well, John Bell may like the psalm, but he doesn't like the way it's been used – or misused, in his view – over the years. And he feels it quite strongly.

JB: It's a psalm which I think is – is greatly misunderstood, because people see it and call it sometime the 'Shepherd Psalm'. That's only one image, and it goes halfway through. Because halfway through it turns to the image of the host. And the image here is very interesting, because the host is the person who lays the table. In every tradition, including Jewish, the person who lays the table is female, so here God is giving us an image of one who leads people, in pleasant places, and one who sets out a meal for them, in which they will be satisfied. So I think a bit of education about Psalm 23 would be a good thing, but just to see it as the kind of things – the kind of thing that you should say or sing at funerals, I think, is totally disrespectful to the psalm.

[26] Rose Hudson-Wilkin likes sheep, and the images the psalm brings up.

RHW: It's this sense of a God who cares that I get from this. A God who doesn't just see us as any other animal, you know. 'You are special', that's what it says to me: 'You are special.' And that

he's going to protect us, he's going to guide us, he's going to pull us back when we go wandering off in directions we shouldn't go in, you know. I love the image. I think it's wonderful.

[27] John goes along with the imagery of sheep and shepherds, but feels we need to understand them for what they are: metaphors.

JB: The psalm is not, you know, demeaning to humanity. And we're not really called sheep in this psalm: it's a metaphor. And the Bible is full of metaphors for God. Sometimes in the psalms he's the lover, sometimes he's the king, sometimes he's a shepherd. There's one psalm which speaks of God as being like a drunk man – or a man who's had too much to drink the night before and is really quite, kind of, irascible in the morning. There's a whole range of images, and these are *metaphors*. You take from the metaphor which is what's applicable, and that is that God wills people, and leads people into pleasant places for their enjoyment, because God wants us to be happy and to be fulfilled. And that's, you know, one of the divine purposes – which doesn't deny the fact that things go wrong.

[28] Timothy thinks the sheep and shepherd images are very helpful in describing what it is to be a Christian.

TR: To be a sheep is to belong to a community. And the community is – certainly in Jesus' times – held together by attentiveness to the voice of the shepherd. So it's to belong to a community, which despite all the temptations to disappear over cliffs and everywhere, stays together. It hears the voice that's addressing them. Now that, it seems to me, is a brilliant description of what it is to be a Christian. It doesn't mean to say we're stupid. It doesn't mean to say that we're brainless. But it does say that we listen to the voice of the shepherd.

[29] *Verse 4 of this psalm talks about the valley of the shadow of death. I asked John if he thought much about his own death.*

JB: Yes I do. And I think that as you get older then that has to be part of the deal. I sometimes think I'd be happy to die tomorrow, because I've had an incredibly privileged and fulfilled life and, you know, if God were, to use the pious term, 'to call me home' tomorrow, I wouldn't object. I mean, I'd miss my friends and the things which here I enjoy, but I think death is part of life, and I regret that – against the advice of a friend of mine who's a lawyer – it's taken me until I was 65 before I wrote my will.

[30] *Timothy gets great comfort from the deaths he witnesses within his community.*

TR: If you've been present with people when they die, then a lot of the fear of death, I think, disappears. We have the tradition in the Order that we always gather round the bed of the brethren when they are dying, and we sing the *Salve Regina*: a beautiful song to Our Lady. Sometimes a brother will open an eye and say: 'isn't this a bit premature?' We had one of our brethren die here – unfortunately I was in South Sudan at the time – but he summoned all the brethren. He renewed his baptismal promises, because he knew he would die later that day. He'd got a bottle of whisky, stored up in the cupboard, which he asked all the members of the community to have a drink with him, and to drink to the resurrection. And then, a couple of hours later, he died. Probably the best sermon he ever preached.

[31] *I wondered where our contributors stood on the issue of assisted suicide.*

RHW: If I'm totally honest with you – and I want to be totally honest – I don't believe in assisted suicide. I have sat with people who are dying, and I think the reason why many people say, you know, we want to have – we want suicide, I think it is because they don't want to be a burden; or, you know, we don't want to look or feel demeaned, or any of those things. So I think the quality of the love that people feel at that time will prevent them saying they want to go down that road. Our human reaction is always: let's not go through the pain – let's find another way of, you know, blanking that bit out. And, I don't want it blanked out, because I believe that God is with me *through* it.

JB: I think that we should consider assisted dying for people for whom – it's not a matter of there being no hope, I mean, if you hope in heaven, then there is always hope. But where – where life is being prolonged, just so that the relatives don't have to deal with a death, I think that that's unfair to the person. And – and we really need to have good conversations with the medical profession about – about when life is being extended against what would be the natural order, and to the detriment of the humanity of the person.

[32] *Timothy isn't so sure.*

TR: I am not yet convinced that this is right. I don't think that doctors should have to go to endless means to perpetuate life. Sometimes the moment has come to die, you know, and treatment should just be stopped. We let somebody – we let somebody die, but to actively intervene to bring about a mature death, as yet I cannot see that this is right. But I have *endless* sympathy with those who do think so.

[33] *For centuries Christians have drawn strength from the hope of heaven, but modern believers seem less confident about glory to come. First from John.*

JB: One of the first funerals I took when I worked in Holland was of an old man who said that he wanted – he knew he was going to die, and he wanted me to preach at his funeral on the text: 'Now I know in part, but then I shall know even as I am known.' And I think to look forward to a place where all the inconsistencies on earth, and all the things that have frustrated us on earth, and all the unanswered questions find the resolution, that's the kind of experience which I believe heaven will give us.

[34] *Rose believes and doesn't worry.*

RHW: I believe in eternal life. Of course I do. I believe that eternal life begins now, with God, and I believe that there is life after death. Perhaps in a different form, I don't know. You know, I don't spend time thinking about it, or

pondering what it might be like. You know, ultimately, God, I'm going to trust you. [*Laughing.*]

[35] *Timothy begins his answer with a bit of a surprise.*

TR: I don't believe in the afterlife. I believe in eternal life – and eternal life begins now. Eternal life begins when you love people, and you forgive them, and you accept their forgiveness. Then you've already begun to live eternally. And that's a life that you will never finish. There was a man called John Rae, who used to be the headmaster of Westminster, and when he was getting on, he began to have to face the fact that he didn't know whether he was a believer or not. With John, it always came down in the end to the question: when he loved people, when he loved his wife, when he loved his children – was that love just a passing emotion? Or did he already enter somehow into something which was transcendent and eternal? Which must endure. And that was the question always with John. He summoned me to his bed just before he died – I was due to fly to Asia the next day – and he said, 'I know you Catholics, you always try and get people on their deathbed – the last minute – but let us talk again about this. Does love endure? Is love ultimately the experience of something transcendent?' And I believe it is. And so the great thing is not a life that happens after you die, it's a life that you begin now.

[36] *In his book* Reflections on the Psalms *C S Lewis writes very disapprovingly about the psalmist's apparent pleasure being made complete, in verse 5, because his enemies must look on while he eats. He calls this gloating 'petty, vulgar and*

contemptible' and yet this is scripture. What can we learn from it? Rose doesn't have any problem with the verse, which she sees as about just deserts.

RHW: Those who don't like us, those who try to destroy us, they will see us thriving because we are God's children. I don't see anything wrong with that. You know, hopefully they may look on and go: 'Wow!' and through that may even be drawn closer to the God who – you know, it's like what God did to the Children of Israel, you know, when – confounded their enemies – you know, led them through the wilderness. And all that. You know, he was there for them, and so those who were once their enemies could see that this is a people who are thriving in the midst of, you know, all that had been thrown, thrown at them.

[**37**] *But John thinks that C S Lewis got it wrong.*

JB: It's a pity that C S Lewis, who himself was a bit of a poet and very useful with language, doesn't see that this is poetic language. You know, it envisaged that, you know, God sets up in front of us all the people who have been hostile towards us, and while they sit behind a glass screen, we enjoy a five-course meal in the best restaurant in London. I mean I think now, come on, I think that – I'd love to ask C S Lewis to reconsider, and to use his poetic understanding to think about these words.

[**38**] *And so, we now hear Jane's reflection on Psalm 23.*

This is a psalm that, more than any other, I have said in the context of death. At funerals and at bedsides, whether said or sung, and whether to the Victorian or contemporary tunes, this psalm has been a friend and dialogue partner for me in the shadow of the valley of death, as I have sought to minister to others and help them to connect with God at the end of their lives, or on the death of their loved ones.

But anything, over-used, can become flat and bland – a mindless comfort – and we can miss its edge, when even the first line of this psalm is actually an extraordinary statement of faith, especially when put into the context of a life that's ending, perhaps prematurely, perhaps in pain, perhaps despite petitions and prayers. 'The Lord is my shepherd I will lack nothing.' The people of Israel often suffered from anxiety about scarcity – remember the manna in the desert? Their ability to trust in the God who would spread a table in the wilderness took some working through, and this is a psalm that shows the workings out, for here is a faith that has been tested in adversity and has endured.

We live in a consumer society, and we still suffer from anxiety about scarcity, hoarding goods as if our lives depended on it. To the extent that I have learned that God is sufficient for the journey, it's through the faith of those whom I've had the privilege to meet at the end of their lives, who were able, even in the face of death, to make this prayer their own.

THE PSALMS Session 4:

PSALM 127 – UNLESS THE LORD BUILDS THE HOUSE...

The old adage says that God helps those who help themselves, whereas the first three verses of this psalm seem to suggest that God helps those who leave it to him. I wondered what our contributors made of that. John Bell, Timothy Radcliffe and Rose Hudson-Wilkin.

JB: I don't think the verses 1 to 3 suggest that God helps those who help themselves. I think verses 1 to 3 suggest that there's a partnership in public things, and that the good that we do, we do in the company of God who inspires that, and who might correct it, and might contradict it. But we don't – we don't go it alone – we're not egocentric. And the glory, you know, has to be something which ultimately is reflected onto our maker, rather than onto our ability.

TR: God does it all. And we do it all. There's no competition. You're really getting off to a bad start if you start saying, 'well, do we leave it to the Lord or do we do it ourselves?' This is to think of God as another actor on the human scene – an extra person. A very powerful one. Which I think is a very deceptive way of looking at God. So I think – we do it – everything is for us to do, but everything is for God to do, because God works in the very deepest part of our own freedom. The closer we are to God, the freer we are.

RHW: God gives us gifts. So he advises us, so we then don't sit on our behinds. We have to get up and get on with it. And so, once or twice, I've stopped – somebody's begged me for money on the street – and I remember one particular incident, where I'd just filled up the gas, and of course I used my card. And a young man looked perfectly well, nothing wrong with him (that I could see), and he begged me for money. And I put my hand in my pocket and I had 50p. And I was embarrassed, because he was a grown man! 'I can't give you 50p,' I said to him. I said, 'Furthermore, what the hell are you doing begging? What's the matter? Talk to me!' You know. 'Oh my, I was living with my girlfriend, and we fall out, and she threw me out.' I said, 'at your age you ought to have your own house. You ought not to be living and depending on somebody else that throws you out of their house!' You know. So, so, I think that we sometimes make the wrong choices in life. And so we need to help ourselves too, by making good choices. And thus enabling – helping ourselves along, along the way. So it's not an 'either or', it's the 'both and'.

[40] Verse 6 declares that those who have a 'quiverful of children' should be happy, but this might be thought to be irresponsible in the light of worldwide population growth, and the accompanying environmental issues of food production, and so on. I put this first to Rose.

RHW: I don't think we should just have children for the sake of having children, without thinking about it. I think we should sit down together and say – before, actually before we get married – I think we should be saying, you know, 'Do you want to have children? And how many children?' 'Well, I actually only want one, or two.' You know – we should be having that discussion. We shouldn't just be having children.

[41] *Pope Francis talks about responsible parenthood, so naturally I asked Father Timothy for his reaction to Psalm 127 verse 5.*

TR: I love big families. But on the other hand it's perfectly true that our little planet is struggling to be sustainable, and we have to – we have to face this question. I don't know what the answer is. I think that each family has to ask itself, what are they called to do. Are they called to raise large families? Some parents have that vocation. And some maybe don't. I don't think you can give some generalised answer and say: everybody has got to have 2.5 children. Pray, and see what the Lord calls us to.

[42] *John thinks we're barking up the wrong tree.*

JB: I don't think that a 'quiverful of children' has anything to do with population control in the *slightest*. You know, it's a piece of poetry and it comes from five or six centuries before Jesus – and that means 26 centuries before us. When people weren't concerned about human population, but where people liked to have big families. And they needed big families, because there was no old-age pension, and so your children were the people who looked after you. So I think, you know, to see this as in some way an indictment against

people who have big families today, and a warning about overpopulating the earth, is to squeeze out of this psalm juice which is not in it.

[43] *If we are so far away culturally, and in so many other ways, from the Bible, how are we to understand or accept it, when so many things in it seem to be, for example, sexist; anti-gay; pro-war? How can this ancient book called the Bible still guide us in the modern world? We'd better ask John how he would defend it against such criticism.*

JB: I don't know that the Bible needs to be defended. I think it has to be explained that what was written in an age when everybody believed the world was flat, will inevitably have things in it which are totally different, and not immediately applicable to the world as we live in it today. I think also that, you know, with regard to, say, women and the gay issue, we have to look at the Bible again. Women – the stories of women in the Bible – particularly in the Hebrew Scriptures, the Old Testament – have largely been untold to congregations, because men chose the lectionary readings. And so a name like a woman called Rizpah, or a woman called Abigail, or a woman called Tamar will hardly be known. And they are among twenty or so heroes – heroines, I should say – of the Jewish faith, whom God raised up to stand against the injustice and the havoc which men were causing. So I don't see the Bible as a book which demeans women. And I think, you know, with regard to the gay issue, that when people believe that five disconnected texts, coming across the centuries from different authors, are a golden thread that shows us that God has some kind of bias against same-sex relationships, we're really misusing the scripture. If we were to spend as much time on what the Bible says about economics, or what the Bible says about ecology, as we have done discussing five verses about people who have same-sex relations, we might have been more vocal after the 2008 debacle with regard to the nation's finances. And we certainly would be more determined to see creation as that which is entrusted into our care, and not see ecology as an option.

[44] *Timothy and Rose take a similar view from different starting points.*

TR: Pope Benedict, for example, said Revelation is God's conversation with humanity. And it's a conversation that goes on over millennia. And as you get immersed in this conversation with God, slowly, your ideas of God are purified. Slowly, you are free from violent ideas about God. And so you see that the earliest revelation portrays God as a warrior, determined to slaughter all his enemies, but in the course of humanity's conversation with God, we finally come to the moment where we're able to speak of God as the one who turns the other cheek, and lets himself be led to death, rather than bring about vengeance. So you've got to see the whole Bible dynamically, as it moves towards the peacefulness of Jesus.

RHW: We mistakenly try to equate the Bible with a novel being written by any known author today. That's not what it is. And so something that was written in a particular context, at a particular time, is going to reflect that time and context. And, so, today we – our responsibility is to reflect on the context that we find ourselves in, and to draw from scripture that which we need in order to help us to truly live as the children of God in today's age.

[45] *Our last couple of questions move away directly from this psalm – indeed any particular psalm – but just returns to the idea of the psalms being, for many people, part of a regular, everyday form of conversation with God – of God slowly revealing himself in the everyday things of life. A sort of prayer, but less direct than intercession. You may have heard of Brother Lawrence, who, many centuries ago, was the cook in his monastic community. He wrote, 'the time of action does not differ from the time of prayer. I possess God as peacefully in the bustle of my kitchen as I do upon my knees before the Holy Sacrament. I turn my little omelette in the pan for the love of God.' I wondered how this domestic image strikes Timothy and Rose.*

TR: Brother Lawrence, no doubt, you know, encountered God in his pots. But I don't think he would have done so if he hadn't also had the silence. You need a life, I think, which has silence *and* pots. And if he hadn't had the pots, he mightn't have also been able to discover God so eloquently in the silence. And we all need days that have rhythm – different sorts of rhythm – where we learn God by reading the papers; we learn God by reading poetry; we learn God by going for a walk or having a nice hot bath, you know – or doing the cooking. So I think it's the very variety of our experiences that enrich our understanding of God.

RHW: It's a lovely image, because it takes from our mind an aloof God, who is in some distant clouds looking down, occasionally intervening, occasionally striking us with, you know, fire and brimstone, etc. And, you know, it takes a God who is warm, friendly, cuddly, but also a God who is to be respected and feared – or feared – and a God who is interested in all our lives, in our everyday lives. And that's the kind of God that I want.

[46] *How comfortable is John with this image of the everyday God?*

JB: It seems almost like domesticating God, you know. Whereas I think 'God everyday' is perhaps a better use of these two words, because we don't know how God will intervene in our lives – how God will turn up, with what God might surprise us. And, and we have to see our maker as more than a, kind of, domestic friend. And when we talk about how God is every day, then that opens us to the wonder that tomorrow might be different from yesterday, and that the profound theological thoughts we have – we've had about God in the past might be surpassed by something different and truer that we'll discover in the future.

[47] *So Jane Leach picks up quite a different theme within this psalm, for her final reflection of the whole course.*

There is much about this psalm that sounds like the kind of conventional faith with which I have difficulty: if you behave well then God will reward you; God will reward you with sons because sons are more valuable than daughters; if in doubt, there's strength in numbers.

If you struggle to identify with a psalm, it's good advice to ask the question: 'Whose prayer is this?' For the most part this seems to be a psalm that affirms the way things are for those whose certainties have not been disturbed; for those whose cities have never fallen; for those whose family life has turned out as planned; and for those who have never needed to burn the candle at both ends to make a living.

Yet, despite my misgivings, I still find myself challenged by the cautionary note sounded in this psalm against the kind of driven-ness that cannot trust to rest or sleep, or to God's care. As a young woman, on the night before leading worship for the first time as a Methodist minister, I was writing and re-writing the text of my sermon into the small hours, for fear of getting it wrong. When I finally got to bed, it was this text that greeted me in the *Order of Night Prayer* compiled by Jim Cotter:

It is lost labour that you haste to rise up early, and so late take rest, and eat the bread of anxiety. For those beloved of God are given gifts even whilst they sleep.

These verses have served as a reminder to me ever since, that the work of entrusting my anxiety to God needs to be a first duty and not a last resort.

The Course Booklet...

... is written and introduced by Bishop Stephen Cottrell, who was consecrated as Bishop of Chelmsford in 2010. Before ordination he worked in the film industry, and for a year at St Christopher's Hospice in Sydenham. A longstanding member of the Governing Body of the College of Evangelists, he is the author of numerous books.

ISBN 978-1-909107-11-3

YORK COURSES

York Courses
PO Box 343
York YO19 5YB UK
T:01904 466516
www.yorkcourses.co.uk
E:info@yorkcourses.co.uk

PARTICIPANTS on the CD

FR TIMOTHY RADCLIFFE OP is Director of the Las Casas Institute, Blackfriars, Oxford and an itinerant preacher and lecturer. He was a Trustee of the Catholic Agency for Overseas Development from 2001 to 2014. He was awarded the Michael Ramsey Prize for theological writing in 2007.

REVD PREBENDARY ROSE HUDSON-WILKIN, BPhil Ed was born and grew up in Montego Bay, Jamaica. In 2007 she was appointed as a Chaplain to Her Majesty the Queen and in 2010, she became the first female Chaplain to the Speaker of the House of Commons.

JOHN BELL is a Resource Worker with the Iona Community, who lectures, preaches and conducts seminars across the denominations. A hymn writer, author and occasional broadcaster, John is based in Glasgow and works with his colleagues in the areas of music, worship and spirituality.

REVD DR JANE LEACH is the Principal of Wesley House, Cambridge, having previously served as a Circuit Methodist Minister. She has published articles and books on theological education, pilgrimage and pastoral supervision, and is a regular broadcaster on Radio 4's *Thought for the Day*.

CANON SIMON STANLEY co-founder of *York Courses* interviews the participants. He is a Canon Emeritus of York Minster and a former BBC producer/presenter.